CW00341335

ARTWORK: KYLE LAMBERT / MUSIC TRANSCRIPTIONS: OLIVER WEEKS / EDITOR: LUCY HOLLIDAY / © 2018 BY FABER MUSIC LTD /
FIRST PUBLISHED BY FABER MUSIC LTD IN 2018, BLOOMSBURY HOUSE, 74–77 GREAT RUSSELL STREET,LONDON WC1B 3DA /
PRINTED IN ENGLAND BY CALIGRAVING LTD / ALL RIGHTS RESERVED / ISBN:0-571-54097-X / EAN13: 978-0-571-54097-6

REPRODUCING THIS MUSIC IN ANY FORM IS ILLEGAL AND FORBIDDEN BY THE COPYRIGHT, DESIGNS AND PATENTS ACT, 1988 /
TO BUY FABER MUSIC PUBLICATIONS OR TO FIND OUT ABOUT THE FULL RANGE OF TITLES AVAILABLE, PLEASE CONTACT YOUR
LOCAL MUSIC RETAILER OR FABER MUSIC SALES ENQUIRIES: FABER MUSIC LIMITED, BURNT MILL, ELIZABETH WAY, HARLOW
CM20 2HX / TEL: +44 (0)1279 82 89 82 FAX: +44 (0)1279 82 89 83 / SALES@FABERMUSIC.COM FABERMUSICSTORE.COM

ALGORITHM

WORDS AND MUSIC BY MATTHEW BELLAMY

Re - - - load,

with your cre - a - - - tor.

THE DARK SIDE

WORDS AND MUSIC BY MATTHEW BELLAMY

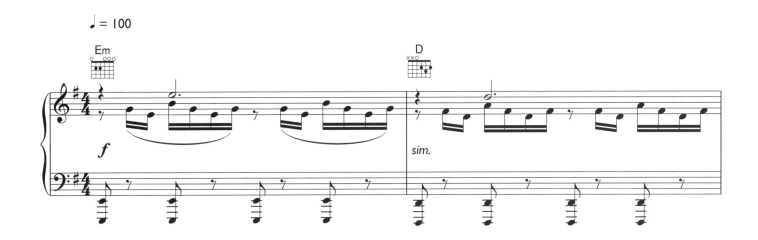

(Yeah, yeah, yeah, yeah, yeah, yeah,____ ah

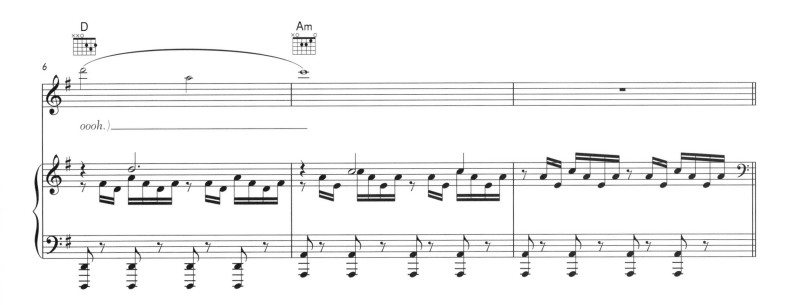

oooh.)____

14

PRESSURE

WORDS AND MUSIC BY MATTHEW BELLAMY

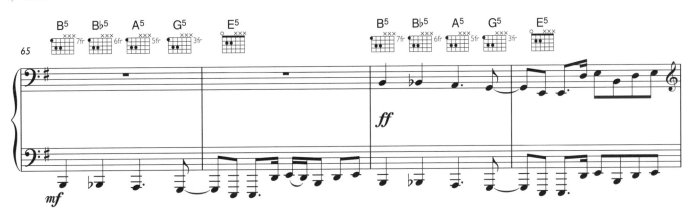

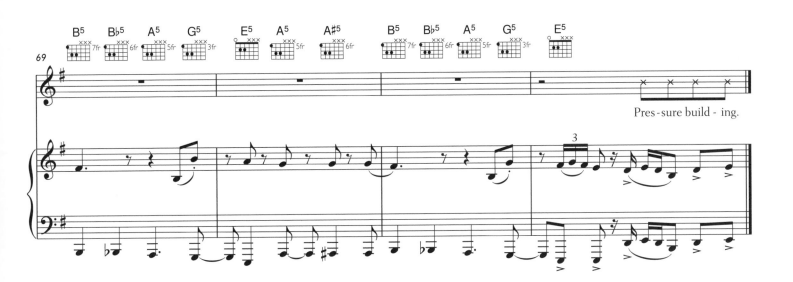

PROPAGANDA

WORDS AND MUSIC BY MATTHEW BELLAMY,
TIMOTHY MOSLEY, ANGEL LOPEZ AND FEDERICO VINDVER

Tune guitar to D minor cross tuning:
1 = D   4 = D
2 = A   5 = A
3 = F   6 = D

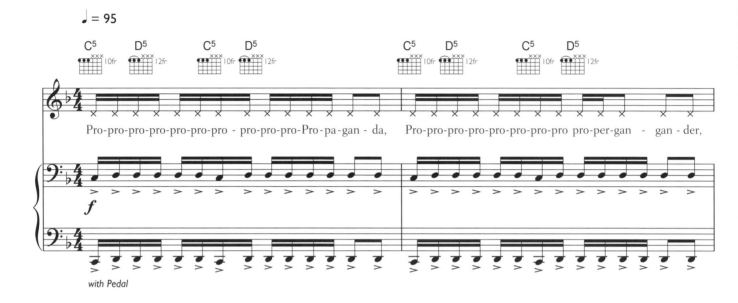

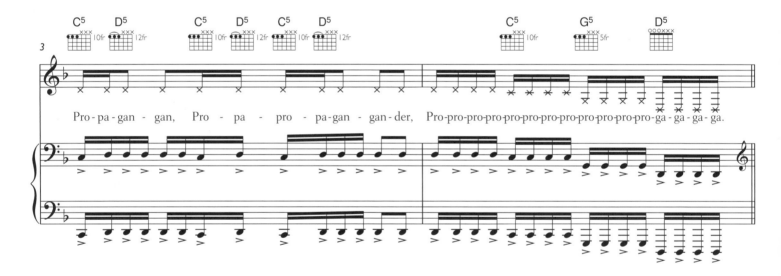

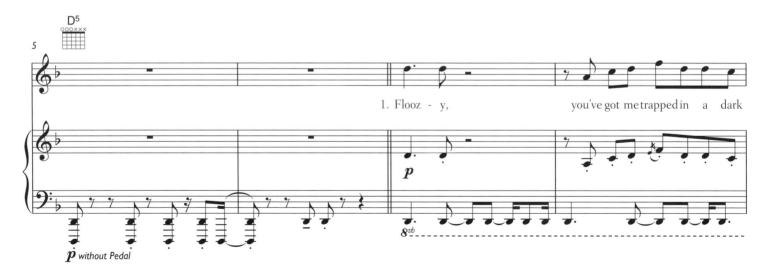

Pro - pa-gan - gan, Pro-pa - pro-pa-gan - gan-der, Pro-pro-pro-pro-pro-pro-pro-pro-pro-pro-pro-pro-ga - ga-ga-ga.

Can't   lose,___   you make me of - fers that I   can't   re - fuse,___

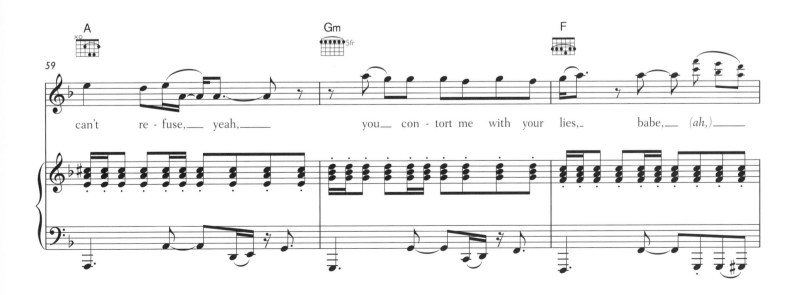

BREAK IT TO ME

WORDS AND MUSIC BY MATTHEW BELLAMY

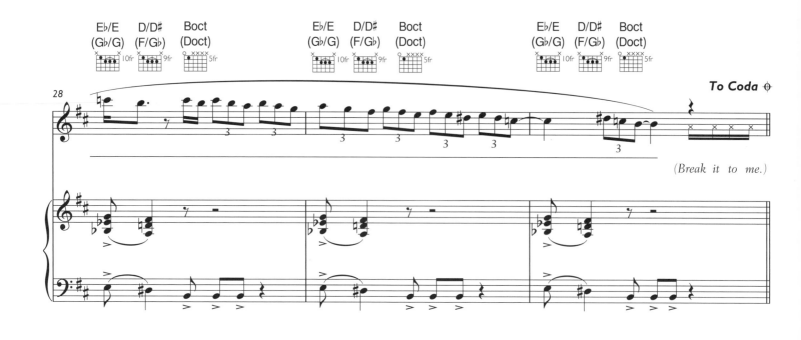

(Break it to me.)

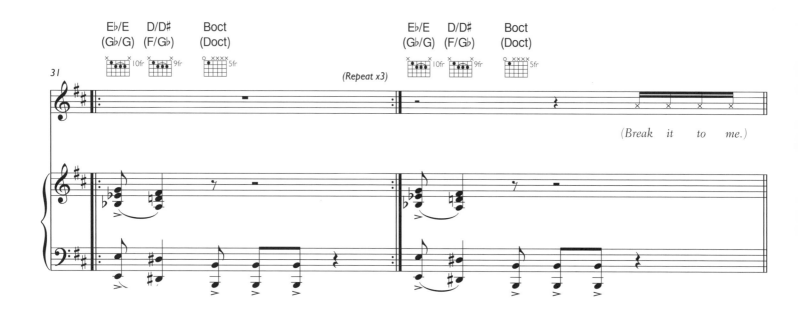

(Break it to me.)

Don't dress it up,___ don't beat a-round the bush and don't cov-er it up,___ don't push it un-der-ground and don't

just break it to me.)

(Guitar FX approximation)

SOMETHING HUMAN

WORDS AND MUSIC BY MATTHEW BELLAMY

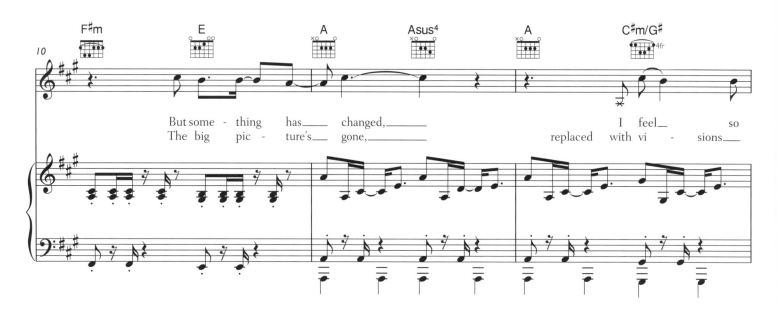

But some - thing has____ changed,_____ I feel____ so
The big pic - ture's____ gone,_____ replaced with vi - sions____

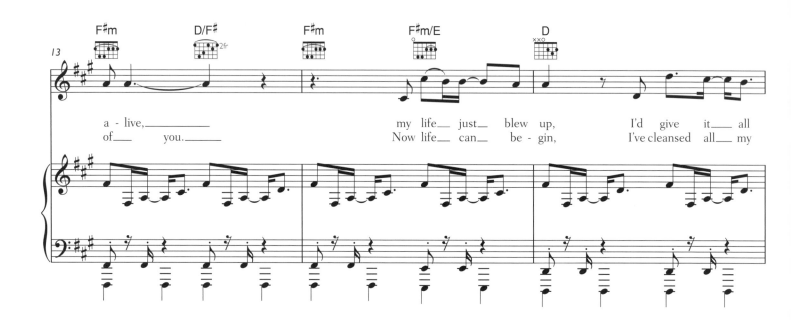

a - live,_____ my life____ just____ blew up, I'd give it____ all
of____ you._____ Now life____ can____ be - gin, I've cleansed all____ my

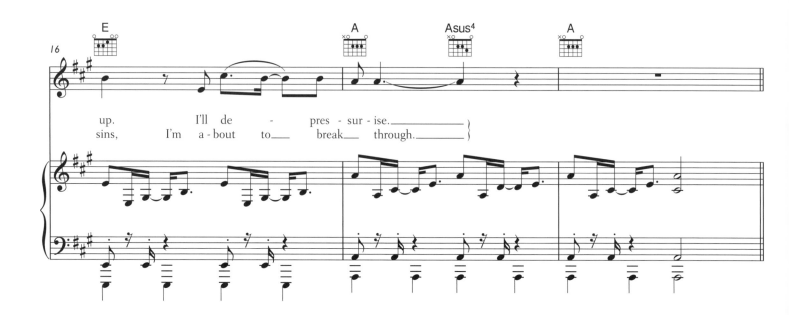

up. I'll de - pres - sur - ise._____ }
sins, I'm a - bout to____ break____ through._____ }

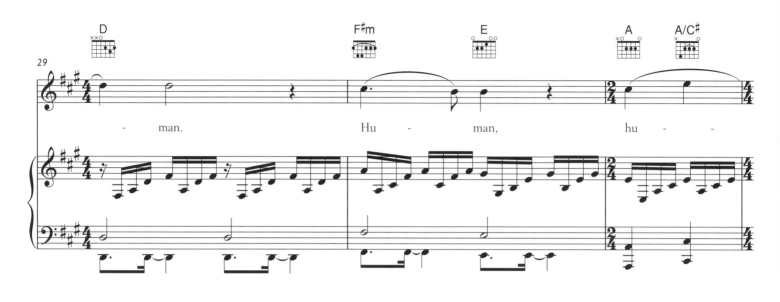

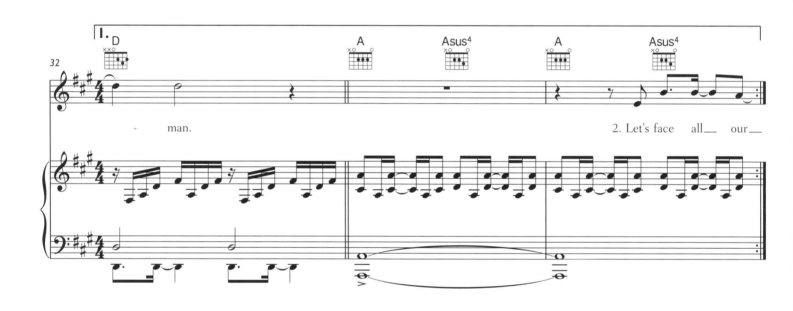

THOUGHT CONTAGION

WORDS AND MUSIC BY MATTHEW BELLAMY

1. Strung out, fall - ing from the big time, wel-come to__ the in - fi-nite black skies.__

Brain__cleansed, frac - tured i - den-ti-ty, frag - ments and scat - tered de - bris.__

GET UP AND FIGHT

WORDS AND MUSIC BY MATTHEW BELLAMY AND JOHAN SCHUSTER

1. What we have's___ the on — ly thing worth fight — ing for___ and I,___
2. In our heads,___ a mil — lion voic — es scream___ and shout but no-

___ I won't let no — thing keep us a — part.___
— one will e — ver hear___ a sound.__ Oh,_____

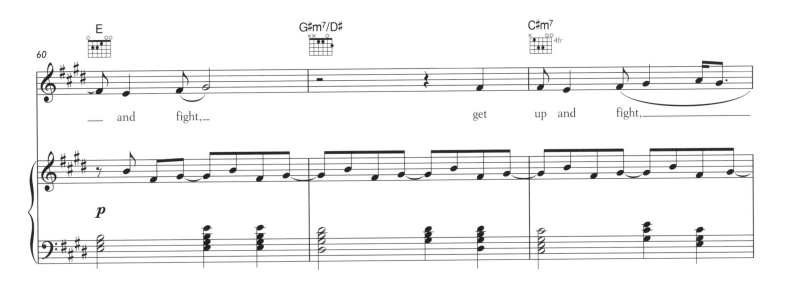

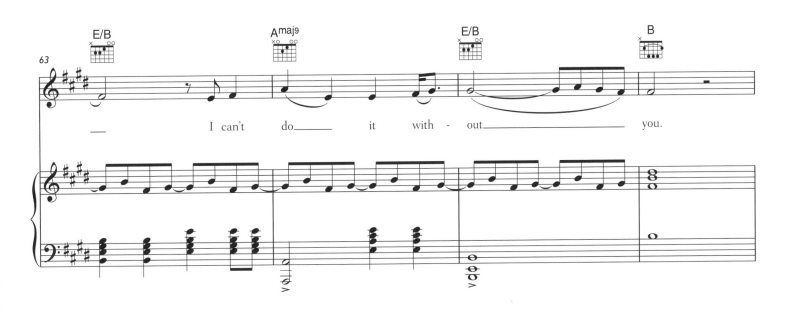

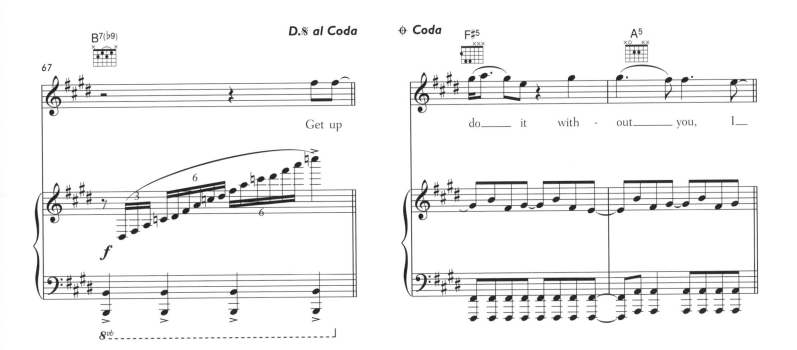

BLOCKADES

WORDS AND MUSIC BY MATTHEW BELLAMY

1. The

DIG DOWN

WORDS AND MUSIC BY MATTHEW BELLAMY

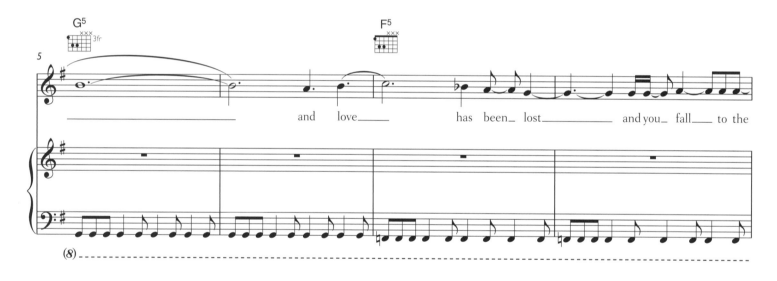

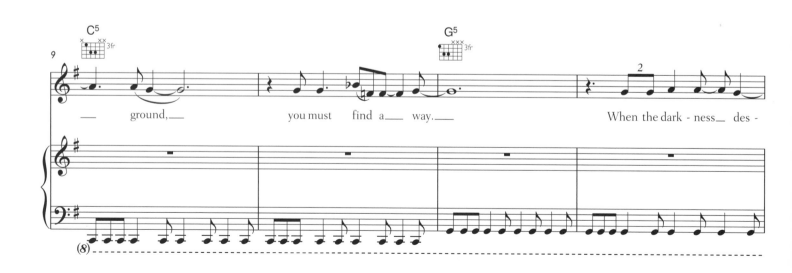

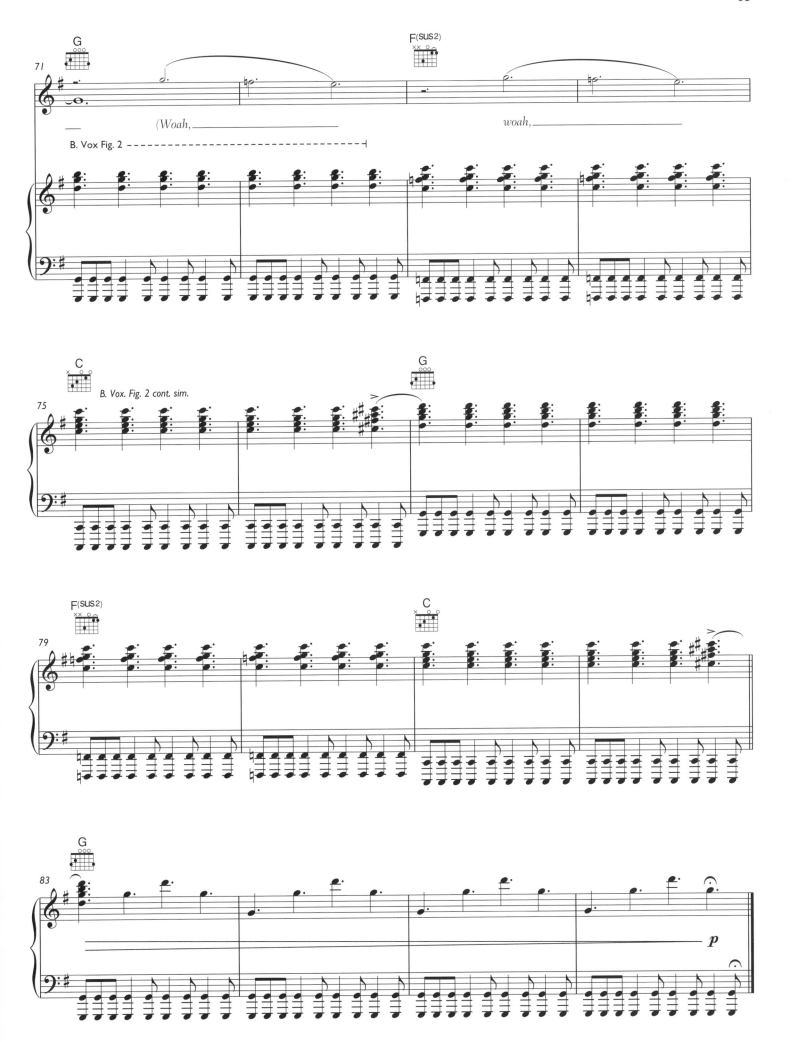

THE VOID

WORDS AND MUSIC BY MATTHEW BELLAMY

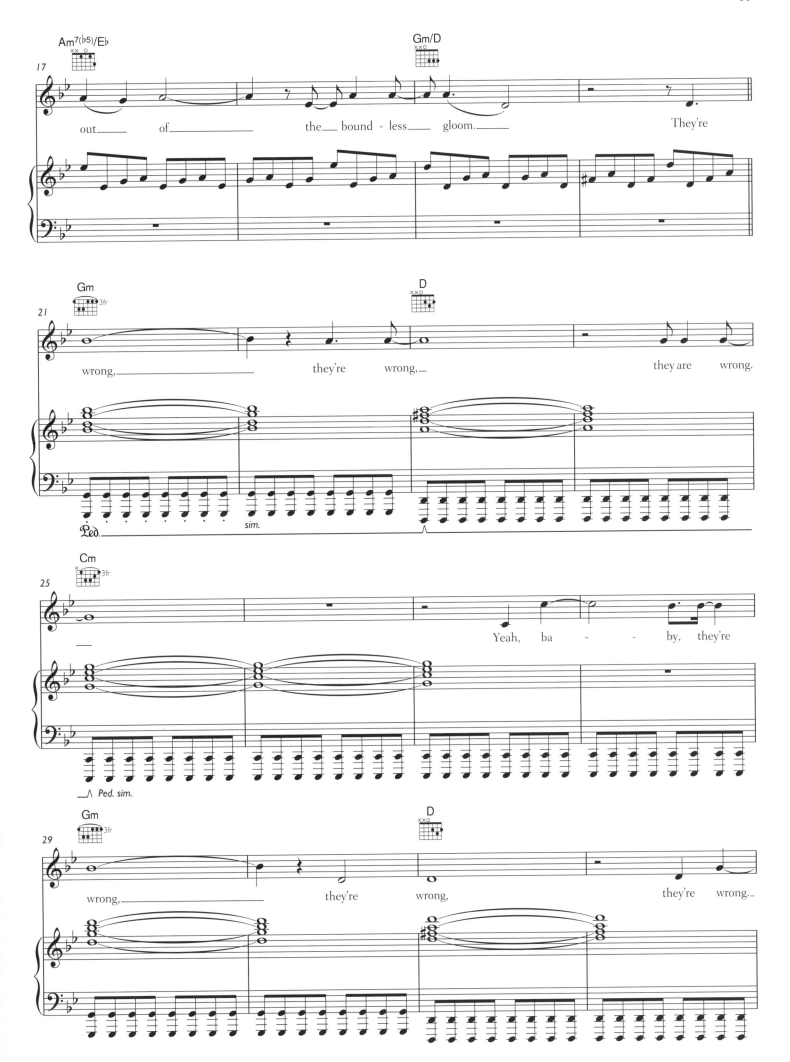